# Ducks in The Henhouse

The Challenges of Integrating Direct and Brand Advertising

First Edition Hardcover, February 2005

ISBN 0-615-12641-3

Printed in the United States of America

# Contents

# Contents

# Contents

# Contents

*Ducks in The Henhouse* tells two stories in one. The first is my story—how I've come to develop the thinking expressed in this book, and how we incorporate that thinking into the way my agency approaches direct advertising. The second is the story of direct and brand advertising—and how to put them together. As I share my vision with you, I promise you a fun read. You'll not only learn how far direct has come, but you'll also get a glimpse of its future.

—Jon Roska

• I •

# The Difference Between Brand Advertising and Direct Advertising

Over the 20 years that I've been in the direct advertising business, new employees, recruits, interns and even clients have often asked me, "What's the difference between brand advertising and direct advertising?" And I'd give them David Ogilvy's classic answer, because Ogilvy wasn't just a leader in brand advertising, he was a leader in direct advertising as well.

According to David Ogilvy, brand is, "The intangible sum of a product's attributes—its name, packaging and price, history, reputation and the way it's advertised."

The *Dictionary of Business and Management* defines brand as, "...a name, sign or symbol used to identify items or services of the seller(s) and to differentiate them from goods of competitors."

But I think Walter Landor really hit the nail on the head: "...a brand is a promise. By identifying and authenticating a product or service, it delivers a pledge of satisfaction and quality."

A brand *is* a promise—a promise a company makes to you when you buy their product or service—a promise that their product or service is going to do what they say it will do.

Now look at how we define "direct marketing."

According to the Direct Marketing Association, "Direct marketing is broadly defined as any direct communication to a consumer or business recipient that is designed to generate a response in the form of an order (direct order), a request for further information (lead generation), and/or a visit to a store or other place of business for purchase of a specific product(s) or service(s) (traffic generation)." Direct must also have an accountable response that can be projected for a return on investment.

What a difference! Direct seems so clinical, while brand seems to have an aura about it—a glow that makes you want to hug a tree or kiss a whale. Sure, direct folks know how to target a response, generate an order, build a database. But where's the love? Well, maybe it's time for us to start thinking about that.

## • II •

# A Simpler Way To Look at It

Often, after explaining the difference between brand and direct, I'd still get blank stares—especially from young interns. So I figured out a way to make the whole explanation simpler.

Think of advertising as a farm. After all, it's hard work requiring long hours. When things get hot, a whole new crop of ideas springs up. And, of course, there's always plenty of manure to spread around.

The farmer is the client. He produces the product. But he needs help selling it. So he turns to his chickens and his ducks. The chickens are his brand marketers. The ducks are his direct marketers. After all, chickens and ducks are both birds. And brand agencies and direct agencies both create advertising. They just approach it in a different way. Brand advertising sells the reputation of the farm. Direct advertising sells the products the farm produces.

## • III •

# Chickens as Brand Marketers

Brand advertising builds awareness. The chickens tell the farmer that he'll generate sales by building a strong brand. They'll create an identity for his farm that customers will remember. They promise him that if they sell his brand successfully, product sales will follow.

Watching the chickens work on his brand advertising, the farmer notices that there's something strange about these birds. They like to speak in parables. The ads they dream up always seem to have headlines with double meanings. And many selling points often fall between the lines. He also notices that the chickens always seem to be having fun. This makes him wonder—are they making ads for him or for themselves?

But—people are beginning to pay attention to the ads. Suddenly, they're aware of the farm and its products.

## • IV •

# Ducks as Direct Marketers

Direct advertising sells products. The ducks now tell the farmer that he shouldn't be selling the farm's image. He should be bringing the farm's brand to life by advertising its products and by developing an ongoing relationship with his customers.

The farmer notices that the ducks aren't anything like the chickens. They don't speak in parables. In fact, they like to point out the obvious, telling the farmer's customers exactly what products the farm has to offer, what those products can do for them, and where to go to get them. What's more, they explain it three different ways, just to make sure that people understand what they're selling and how to get it.

"I'm a duck!"

• V •

# How To Know If You're A Duck

If you have any doubts about whether or not you're a duck, all you need to do is answer the following questions:

- Do you test?
- Is your advertising accountable?
- Do you project ROI?
- Do you use databases?

If you answered "yes" to each of these questions, you're a duck. I'm a duck, too. But if you're not doing all of the above, you're just mailing advertising.

## • VI •

# Chickens Are Chickens. Ducks Are Ducks.

Over the years, I've received many calls from either large brand-oriented agencies or companies doing solid brand advertising telling me that they've been hearing more and more about this "direct marketing." They'd ask about databases...ROI...calls to action... accountability. They'd say, "We'd like to talk to you about it, Jon, because we think we'd like to do some of it, too."

Unfortunately it's not that easy. Chickens are chickens. Ducks are ducks. No matter how I tried to get them to work together, they couldn't or wouldn't. As I watched the feathers fly, I drew some conclusions from what I saw...

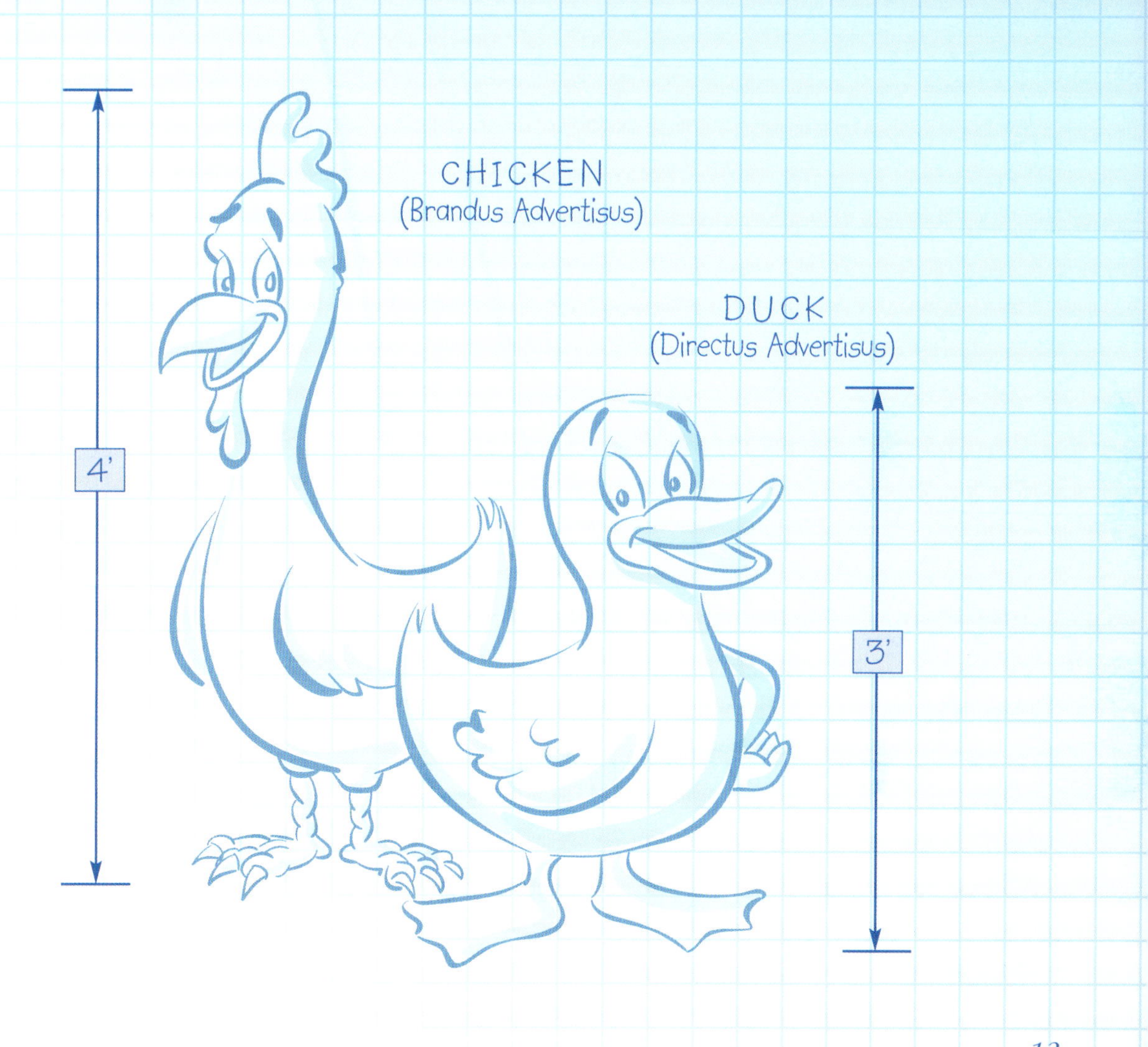
CHICKEN
(Brandus Advertisus)
DUCK
(Directus Advertisus)
4'
3'

## • VII •

# Ducks Who Want To Be Chickens

Sometimes a duck wants to be a brand marketer. He spends his days out on the pond watching the chickens running around, having a great time—enjoying life on the brand side doing all those cutesy, clever, creative ads.

One day, the duck breaks down and decides to give it a try. He goes over to the henhouse and tells the chickens that he'd like to be a brand marketer. The chickens welcome him and celebrate his arrival. "C'mon in, there's always room for another chicken!"

At first, the duck is happy in the henhouse. Until he starts asking questions. Questions you just don't ask chickens: "How much can the farmer make by running this ad?"..."What kind of response are we going to get?"..."Where's the customer database?"

The chickens now realize that they're dealing with a direct marketer. When the duck finally asks them how they'll know if their campaign is successful, that's it! He's out the door!!!

So the duck returns to the pond and his life as a direct marketer—never to engage in such foolish behavior again.

BRAND
FORMULA
BRAND
ABC's

## • VIII •

# Ducks Who Were Raised by Chickens

Ducks who were raised by chickens can become some of our finest direct marketers. These ducks are usually young people who enter a brand advertising agency right out of school. Soon, they become frustrated and unfulfilled. Something very important seems to be missing from their lives. Something called *accountability*. They need to know that their advertising is working—making a profit for the client. But try as they might, they can't prove it—for the client or for themselves.

The lucky ducks read a book or an article on direct advertising and marketing or are spotted by other ducks who pluck them from the brand ranks and find them proper homes on the pond. Of course, whenever we hire one of these wayward ducks, we have to take them into the back room and beat the living hell out of them. It's kind of a de-programming event. Then we retrain them in direct technique—a transition that makes them direct marketers on steroids, über-ducks!

Ducks who aren't fortunate enough to know where they belong face years of therapy, trying to figure out why they're still the only ones in their agency who are interested in results.

Duck
Advertising

## • IX •

# Chickens Who Need A Duck's Help

Sometimes the chickens get wind of the fact that the farmer has been talking to the ducks about direct advertising. Naturally this makes the chickens very nervous. They certainly don't want to lose the account to a bunch of dirty ducks. So they decide to make the farmer happy by inviting a duck over to the henhouse. They promise the farmer that he'll now have the best of both worlds—brand *and* direct advertising.

The chickens kick things off by hosting a big meeting with the farmer and the ducks. This is always a very good meeting, because everyone is all smiles and lovey-dovey. Especially the chickens.

When the meeting ends, the farmer is convinced that everyone's going to work together as a team. He's finally going to get some of that direct advertising he's been hearing so much about! But the second he's out the door, all smiles disappear. The chickens shut the duck up and continue to do the farmer's advertising their way. The last thing they want is accountable advertising.

Chicken
Advertising

SOLD
DUCK
POND

Naturally, the duck is frustrated. And once the farmer sees that he's still not getting accountable advertising, he becomes frustrated, too. Suddenly, the account is in jeopardy. So the chickens do the only thing they can think of when all else fails—they acquire a duck pond they can call their own.

Of course the chickens think this is a stroke of genius. They now have their very own pond to play with. But then, unable to help themselves, the chickens try to turn the direct agency into a brand agency. This leads to pond deterioration. Once again, the farmer doesn't get what he needs.

## • X •

# Chickens in Duck Clothing

Working with ducks didn't work. Buying a duck pond didn't work. Now what are the chickens going to do?

They look around and find one of their own who has shown "duck tendencies." They know he's the one because they found a copy of Stan Rapp's *Maxi Marketing* in his desk drawer. On another occasion, while out with a client, he drank one too many rum and cokes. Everyone heard him ask the client, "What do you think the results of the new campaign will be?"

So they dress him up to look like a duck. Then they march him into the farmer's office. Here he spouts all the right buzz words and, with the rest of the chickens, creates a direct campaign that usually ends up being a disaster.

HA HA HEE
HEE HA HA
DUCK COSTUME

Fed up with yet another chicken ploy, the farmer goes out and does what he should have done in the first place. He hires a genuine direct advertising agency.

Now he has the best of both worlds. Chickens and ducks. Brand and Direct. Working together. Side-by-side.

**Not a chance!**

## • XI •

# Can Chickens and Ducks Work Together?

As I mentioned earlier, many brand agencies acquire direct agencies. Some are very good, but most just mail advertising or put "800" numbers on self-mailers. These captive direct shops are often referred to by their owners as "below the line" agencies. Definitely not free-range ducks!

Roska Direct was acquired by a large, regional, brand agency many years ago. It didn't take long for pond deterioration to set in. I'll never forget one of their top creative directors saying to me, "Jon, everything you do goes against everything I've been taught." The only way I could answer him was, "I know." Right after that we bought our freedom back.

Money is another reason brand and direct agencies don't work well together. Because clients usually take money from the brand budget and put it into the direct budget. They don't expand their ad budget, they simply reallocate it—and that can really upset the chickens.

I remember a client meeting where a brand agency VP was so rude to us that the client had to take him aside and tell him to chill out. We just sat there smiling. And why not? We had just taken 40% of the brand agency's budget. Now, I'm not bragging. I really do make an effort to be part of the team, happy to sit in the circle, holding hands and singing *Kumbaya.*

Your best direct marketers embrace direct marketing as a "philosophy." By philosophy, I mean the "Funk & Wagnalls" definition: "The general laws that furnish the rational explanation of anything." That's why they don't work well with brand marketers (and vice-versa). To a duck, there's no logic to delivering a marketing communication that doesn't have a call to action and an accountable, trackable response! To a duck, there's no logic in marketing to people who are never, ever, going to buy your product.

The vast majority of companies have a very specific customer for their product. New mothers buy diapers. Pet owners buy pet food. Office managers buy copiers. There is a finite number of customers for a product. It could be as small as several thousand for some products like ballet shoes, to many millions, like sneakers.

This is why ducks and chickens often don't work well together. It's not a professional issue. It's a philosophical issue. Good direct marketers will never accept something that goes against "the general laws that furnish the rational explanation of anything!"

## • XII •

# Bringing Brand Thinking To Direct Advertising

The purpose of this book is *not* to teach brand marketers or direct marketers how to work together. We've seen that's rarely possible. What *is* possible, however, is for all of us ducks to get together and apply branding techniques to our own work for our clients and our companies.

Direct marketers classically reject the brand as the key to sales. Many times I've said to a prospective client, "If I make them aware of you, I can't guarantee they'll buy, but if I get them to buy, I guarantee they'll be aware of you."

It's not unusual to work side-by-side with a brand shop. When that shop is the lead agency, we incorporate the brand look into the direct advertising we create. We know for a fact that when we target an audience under a powerful brand, we get a much better response.

When I began to point this out to my fellow direct marketers, I was threatened with expulsion from the pond. I was showing "chicken tendencies." I don't blame them for thinking that way. Then I told them the story of my awakening—my epiphany!

We had been doing all the subscription marketing for a national publication for North American manufacturers. For years, we mailed millions of direct mail packages. In the upper left corner of the envelope, we put the name of the subscription manager with the return address. We thought that having a name there might make the mailing more personal. Although we often modified the package, that name on the return address always remained the same.

One day, the subscription manager went to pick up a part for his motorcycle from its manufacturer. In the process of paying with his credit card, the employee saw his name and hollered to the other employees, “Hey everybody, it’s him, the subscription manager!” Several employees then came over to meet him. They felt they knew him because they had been receiving mail from him for years. That’s when the light went on in my head. That little return address with his name on it was driving awareness! Through reach and frequency, we were turning his name into a brand without even trying!

If I could deliver brand "awareness" and generate direct "response" couldn't I, over time, improve my client's or employer's sales more than if I just did one without the other? I think so. I also think that we owe it to our clients and employers to do both. Because that's the future of branded direct.

But most direct marketers aren't trained to know what makes a brand a brand. So how can we be expected to inject brand into our work? Should we work closely with brand marketers to help us figure it out? I don't think so. We've already seen what happens. We simply have to learn it ourselves.

I believe that it's a lot easier for direct marketers to incorporate good brand thinking than it is for brand marketers to incorporate good direct thinking. Ducks have the edge, and smart ducks will quickly discover that adding the power of "brand" to their work means more than just prettying up a direct campaign with white space and pictures. And smart chickens will find that there's a lot more to direct than just adding an "800" number on the ad.

DIRECT
+ BRAND
GREAT
RESULTS!
E=Mc²

RESULTS
ROI

I'm convinced that brand-based testing must be done over time. Most direct marketers continue to make the mistake of judging their work in the now—looking for an immediate accountable response. But wouldn't it be reasonable to assume that if we were able to build brand while generating response, we would generate a greater response over a longer period of time? To find this out, brand-based direct must be tested long term, using multiple carriers while testing against pure, product-offer direct. This approach will help us prove to our clients or companies that in the long haul, proper brand delivery will improve response.

Also: Every direct marketer worth his salt knows that we generate a lot more sales than we can prove. I've done brand-based direct TV in a market where we generated moderate response to our call to action but increased the product's total share by a point. And that's a lot of money! Consumers who see a direct advertising communication do one of three things. They respond by phone, web, mail or whatever. Or they go purchase the product at a store or point of sale. Or they do nothing, but remain aware of the product. The key to brand-based direct is to take credit for the secondary response and the increased awareness. To do that, it's important to define how results are going to be evaluated.

We once mailed three million direct mail packages for a client and the client's white mail (orders that come in outside of the direct mail package response channel) quadrupled. The client refused to give us credit for those orders. "How do we know the direct mail package was responsible?" they asked.

Those guys were hardcore ducks, and if we didn't have a key code on it to prove it came from the direct mail, they just weren't going to give us credit for the orders. This example may be extreme, but over the years I've seen many instances of this type of thinking. Direct marketers are often their own worst enemies. They claim that they want to be judged by results, yet they ignore all the orders outside of the response channel—all those extra orders for which you're not getting credit that were generated by your advertising.

This is why we encourage our clients to do awareness and purchase intent research before and after a direct campaign "...within the target market!" We have developed formulas that take into account the non-trackable sales (or share within the target market).

Today's direct marketers are in a position to accomplish what traditional agencies have been trying to do for years—turn brand advertising into ROI performance advertising. And we can start by learning to identify and incorporate five key components into the direct advertising we create.

## Incorporate these 5 key components

1. Know the brand's reputation, promise and vision (what we at Roska Direct call RPV).
2. Focus the brand. Focus the target market.
3. Make the internet work twice as hard to help you drive response and build brand.
4. Blend memory triggers with response triggers.
5. Incorporate the brand vision into customer relationship marketing.

## • XIII •

# Know The RPV of Your Brand

The essence of a company's brand can be found in its RPV—reputation, promise and vision. As we move forward, this is what we have to focus on as direct marketers. Any company that's been in business a while has a reputation. Hopefully it's a good one. But if you're starting up a new company, you have to be especially conscientious about building your reputation. About knowing what you stand for and what you believe in.

The brand promise focuses on the product's features. It's what customers expect from your product or service when they buy it.

Finally, there's the brand vision. The brand vision focuses on the product benefits. It's what the customer expects to be or become through the brand, i.e., happier, better looking, higher status.

A simple way to relate Reputation, Promise and Vision to your own life is:

**R**eputation is how we get somebody to go out on a date with us.

**P**romise is how we get them to marry us.

**V**ision is how we go on to raise a family.

And here's another way to look at where to emphasize each component of the RPV in a customer continuum.

• XIV •

# Focus The Brand.<br>Focus The Target Market.

Several years ago I was visiting one of my clients. Toward the end of the meeting, the client, a very bright woman and an outstanding direct marketer, handed me a book titled, "The 22 Immutable Laws of Branding" by Al Ries and Laura Ries.

I remember laughing when she handed me the book and commenting that I was surprised that a book on branding was even allowed in a company that was so focused on direct marketing.

The book sat on my desk for many months, unopened, slowly being buried under a pile of papers and unopened mail.

One day I noticed a corner of the book peeking out from under the pile. I pulled it out and opened it up to a random page.

It must have been fate. Right there in front of me was a headline that said, "A brand becomes stronger when you narrow its focus."

I was intrigued as I read through the authors' explanation of this concept. They said there were thousands of coffee shops selling breakfast and lunch, sandwiches, soups and sodas. But one company created a megabrand coffee shop by focusing on one thing—coffee.

Instantly I made the connection with something that I'd known from my direct marketing career —response becomes stronger when you focus your target audience.

Consider this example.

At the height of the dotcom start-up era, a small pet product company, with Duck marketers, had a meager amount of venture capital but a lot of direct marketing know-how. They sat on the sidelines while the giant competition, with Chicken marketers, ran commercials on the Super Bowl.

The Ducks' game plan was to create a best buyer profile and concentrate their limited marketing dollars to reach only those prospects that fit that profile—not the 150+ million people who were watching the Super Bowl. They knew early on that one of the keys to success would be a high average order amount, so they focused on multi-pet households. They also knew that with their scant marketing budget, they couldn't get a significant share of voice nationally, so they focused on a geographic region where over 20% of the pet owning households lived—the Northeast corridor from Boston to Richmond, VA. They focused the target market and built the business one customer at a time from the pool of best buyer prospects while the giant competition burned through more than $100 million promoting to an unfocused market.

The result: Chickens out of business; Ducks still in business and growing. The marketer that focused the brand and the target audience triumphed over the marketer who didn't.

Something else to always be aware of is that there are multiple segments within every prospect and customer market. Where a customer is within his or her life cycle can have a dramatic impact on how that individual perceives the brand.

These customer perceptions can be grouped into marketing segments.

Consumers in each of these segments relate to the brand on a different level because each has a different need. For example, let's look at a cleaning product:

- To the 27-year-old, the brand is a new friend that helps her around the house
- To the 43-year-old, the brand is a trusted housekeeper, keeping her home clean
- To the 57-year-old, the brand is an old friend who's always there

Focus your brand so that you make it stronger. Clearly establish its reputation, its promise and its vision. Identify your best buyer profile and determine the best way to hone in on your target market so that you're reaching your best prospects.

Direct marketers have an advantage in combining these concepts. They already know how to focus on the target audience. What we need to do is embrace the concept of focusing the brand. Because once we deliver the brand reputation, promise and vision to the targeted market, speaking to the target market to the exclusion of all others, we will accomplish what the brand agencies have failed to provide for their clients: accountable advertising that delivers the brand and generates a response.

So put the two concepts together:

**Focus the brand on a targeted market and you hit a home run!**

# • XV •

## Make The Internet Work Twice As Hard

Study after study has shown that the internet can build your brand, but to just use the internet to build brand is a waste of such an interactive medium. At the same time, using the internet to only sell a product or generate a lead is not taking advantage of the awareness you can build for your brand. *Do both at the same time.*

If you're running banner ads, use the colors, logos and visuals that match your print, direct mail or TV. When someone clicks on your banner ad, make sure that they go to landing pages that complement the offer and look of your brand. One of the biggest mistakes I see is when marketers create interactive ads that take the responder to the front page of their website...leaving the prospect trying to figure out where to go on the site to find what was promised in the interactive ad.

I'm always amazed at how many companies separate their interactive marketing from the rest of the marketing department. These companies create TV commercials, print ads and direct mail in their marketing department and then have the technology department create the web advertising! Technology departments don't "create" web advertising; they "build" web advertising. Companies that separate interactive from the rest of their marketing mix deserve the uncoordinated pablum they produce and the poor results they generate.

## • XVI •

# Blend Memory Triggers With Response Triggers

As direct marketers, we all know about response triggers—words like free, act now, call now, click here, etc., or attention-getting visuals that pull the eye to the product or offer, like bursts or coupons. But as direct advertising moves into the future, we need to leave our customers with more than just an offer. We need to incorporate the memory triggers that branding shops have been using for years. We need to incorporate the colors, shapes, music and taglines that make a brand a brand—the sum total of everything that leaves an impression on our customers.

We can no longer afford to think about our marketing approach as simply a way to get a response. Of course, you'd like to get one. But if you don't, it's not the end of the world. Because you'll get it the next time—as long as you're conscientious about leaving your prospect with memory triggers that lead to a sale.

Remember: It's a new day for direct marketers. We shouldn't be judged just by what kind of response we can generate the first time we do a campaign. Or worse yet, on the first piece that goes out and the ROI it produces. We need to do double duty now—blending brand and direct—to win the long game. And memory triggers can help.

BUY NOW!

• XVII •

# Incorporate Brand Vision Into Customer Relationship Marketing

If you're a leader, you have a vision you can share with others. When others buy into your vision, they'll follow. They may even become advocates for your vision. That's Management Training 101. But it also applies to marketing. As I pointed out earlier, a brand must have a vision, too—a vision customers must buy into in order for the brand to grow.

The product satisfies a customer need. The brand satisfies a customer vision: what they want to do, where they want to go, who they want to be.

When a brand can meet the goal, emotion, or aspiration of the customer, only then will customer loyalty, retention, and advocacy be achieved.

This isn't something that comes easily to direct marketers. After all, we're used to selling cars, food, all kinds of products and services. But if we can train ourselves to incorporate brand vision into our advertising, we'll be doing a better job for everyone involved.

# • XVIII •

# Why Technology Puts Direct Advertising Light Years Ahead

Technology has already begun to give direct marketers the edge over brand advertisers. For over 20 years I've watched and participated in the pursuit of the Holy Grail of direct advertising: "A personal, one-on-one communication with the consumer." This concept requires unique marketing communications at every stage of the customer continuum. But until recently, data and communication technology were expensive and cumbersome. Every time we would try to implement this type of marketing, it was usually successful in the testing phase, but failed as the campaigns grew. That's because data technology, up to several years ago, penalized you for growing your database. Updates, cleaning and input could cost \$.25 to \$.50 a record. On a 5-million record database, you could easily spend \$1.2 to \$2.5 million building and maintaining it. Then you have to add the marketing costs—because if you're going to build a database, you might as well use it!

The cost of entry into high-level data marketing was terrifying to someone who had never done it before. And what made it even more terrifying was that the results of your marketing were right there for you and everyone else to see—so they had to be good.

Today, technology allows us to automate most of the customer management process. And in many cases, the customer can now maintain his or her data in the system. No longer do we need to be penalized for doing a good job and growing our customer and prospect files. This can open up unlimited opportunities.

Let me share a secret: Anything you can imagine, technology can build. Techies are just waiting for somebody to challenge them with the next big idea. But there are some hurdles you have to overcome to get them onboard. The first and highest hurdle you have to deal with is the "technology mantra": *"We don't have the time. We don't have the budget. We don't have the resources."* All technology personnel emerge from the womb able to recite this. They don't really mean it. It's just something they have to say. But when they realize you're not buying it, they'll issue an even bigger roadblock: *"What you want to do is impossible."*

The key to clearing this hurdle is to understand that what technophiles mean when they say "impossible" is simply that it's never been done before. They're not saying that they can't figure out a way to make the impossible happen! So ignore this response, too. And remember, if you're going to let lack of time, budget, and resources—or the fact that something is impossible—get in the way of a big, hairy idea, you might as well get out of the business now. Face it, there's never enough time, budget or resources. And lots of great ideas were impossible until technology finally figured them out.

ROBO

THE NEW
DIRECT
ADVERTISIN
DICTIONARY

• XIX •

# Redefining Direct Advertising

At the risk of having The Direct Marketing Association put out a contract on me, I've taken it upon myself to propose a new definition for direct advertising: **Direct advertising is broadly defined as a direct communication designed to deliver the brand reputation, promise and vision to a consumer, and generate a response in the form of an order (direct order), a request for further information (lead generation), and/or a visit to a store or other place of business to purchase a specific product(s) or service(s) (traffic generation) while building brand awareness in the target audience.**

This, I believe, is where direct advertising is headed. So do many others in our industry. But I've only pointed to a direction here—the coming together of brand and direct.

Although I've given you a number of ideas on how to incorporate brand advertising into direct advertising efforts, I'm sure there are many, many more. At the least, I hope I've given enough to start you thinking. Change is our only constant, and where we go from here is up to all of us.

• XX •

# In Conclusion

"Ducks in The Henhouse" has given me the opportunity to travel throughout the world giving presentations to large groups of people in the advertising and marketing fields. A common complaint among the marketing heads of many companies is how difficult it is to coordinate and work with multiple agencies. Remember what I said earlier about budget conflict? Well, integrated advertising is the battleground. Integrated advertising requires the client to be expert in all marketing disciplines—otherwise, the client will not be able to effectively coordinate, communicate and manage his advertising.

Integrated advertising was developed by the large agency holding companies to slow or stop the bleed of budget dollars that started moving to independent direct, promotion and interactive agencies in the early 90s. By acquiring these "Below the Line" agencies the holding companies were able to offer integrated services that promised the advertiser less hassle and more efficiency. It sounded like a good idea, but in reality, integrated agency services simply kept the budget in the holding company while the client continued to have to manage the holding company's multiple agencies. End result, no improvement for the client.

I once had the good fortune of being with a group of direct agency presidents that Stan Rapp was addressing. Mr. Rapp was asked by an agency head, "What is the advertising agency of the future?" He answered, "There won't be brand agencies or direct agencies, there will be marketing agencies."

The marketer/advertiser/agency of the future must be expert in brand and direct. Not as two separate disciplines, but as one new discipline that merges the best of both. This solves the integration problem by replacing it with a better type of marketing.

If I may be so bold, I have taken the liberty to call this new marketing Fusion Marketing. It's certainly not an original term, but my definition is more than a catchy word for what is really integrated marketing. Let's go to "Funk and Wagnalls" and get the real definition of Fusion.

- A melting or blending together
- A thermonuclear reaction in which the nuclei of a light element undergo transformation into those of a heavier element, with the release of great energy

The first bullet says it all, but the second bullet describes it with passion. Now let's put it all together.

## Fusion Marketing

Brand and direct, two separate marketing elements, coming together to undergo a transformation into a new element. With the release of great energy!

I'm often asked if a duck can turn into a chicken, or vice-versa. I've given this a lot of thought and the answer is no. Whenever a direct or brand marketer thinks they have moved to the other discipline, they are mistaken. By becoming an expert of both brand and direct, they become something totally different. They become a Fusion Marketer.

Everyone I talk to wants me to represent a Fusion Marketer as some sort of combination duck-chicken. I've had suggestions ranging from "Chucks" to "Duckens."

But none of these suggestions represent the power of what a Fusion Marketer can do.

Fusion Marketers will deliver the brand and generate an accountable response. Fusion Marketers will be in high demand because they can deliver the solution to the problem advertisers are crying their eyes out about. Fusion Marketers will make a lot of money for the companies they work for and themselves.

What better representation of the Fusion Marketer than the goose that lays the golden egg!